PHILIPPIANS
Joy in Christ

Rejoice in the Lord always.
I will say it again: Rejoice!
Philippians 4:4

By Julene Gernant Dumit

CPH.
SAINT LOUIS

Series editors: Thomas J. Doyle and Rodney L. Rathmann

We solicit your comments and suggestions concerning this material. Please write to Product Manager, Adult Bible Studies, Concordia Publishing House, 3558 S. Jefferson Avenue, St. Louis, MO 63118-3968.

Scripture taken from the HOLY BIBLE, NEW INTERNATIONAL VERSION®. NIV®. Copyright © 1973, 1978, 1984 by International Bible Society. Used by permission of Zondervan Publishing House. All rights reserved.

Contents

Lesson 1

Partners in the Gospel (Philippians 1:1-11)

Theme Verses

"In all my prayers for all of you, I always pray with joy because of your partnership in the gospel from the first day until now" (**Philippians 1:4–5**).

Goal

We seek to put our confidence in God who began the good work of salvation in us and will bring it to completion. We seek to pray with joy as did Paul for our partners in the Gospel that their love, informed by knowledge of God's will revealed in His Word, might result in God being glorified.

What's Going On Here?

Paul had a warm and close relationship with the people of Philippi. We will look at the history of that relationship and then at the opening of Paul's letter to the Philippians. In that opening Paul points them to God's gracious working in their lives and prays for their continued growth in holy living.

Searching the Scriptures

Philippi (named after Philip II, the father of Alexander the Great) was located in eastern Macedonia, in what is today part of Greece. At the time of Paul, Philippi was a Roman colony. As a Roman colony, the affairs of Philippi were managed as if Philippi were in Italy. The citizens of Philippi were also Roman citizens. Rome settled many veterans in Roman colonies such as Philippi, thus placing loyal citizens in strategic spots throughout the empire. The Egnatian Way, the main road between Rome and the East, past through Philippi.

The apostle Paul first visited Philippi in around A.D. 51 on his second missionary journey. It was there that he planted the first Christian congregation on European soil. Read about Paul's visit in **Acts 16:6–40**. You might want to consult a biblical map showing Asia Minor and Macedonia to locate the places mentioned in **16:6–12**.

1. Why did Paul go to Macedonia?

Paul's usual practice was to first go to the synagogue to proclaim the Gospel to those gathered there—Jews and Gentiles who worshiped God **(Acts 13:14; 14:1; 17:1–3)**. Apparently there were so few Jews living in Philippi that there was no synagogue. So on the Sabbath, Paul and his companions went to the river where they expected to find a place of prayer.

2. Who were among those who believed the Gospel, were baptized, and thus became members of the church in Philippi? Note that in **16:10** Luke, the author of Acts, uses the pronoun *we*, indicating that he was among Paul's companions who accompanied him to Macedonia. According to **16:1–3** who also was among Paul's companions?

Apparently Luke stayed behind in Philippi when Paul and Silas were asked to leave, because he doesn't use first-person pronouns *(we, us)* again until **Acts 20:6**, when Paul and his companions were again departing from Philippi after a later visit.

The believers in Macedonia sent support for Paul's later ministry when he was in Corinth **(2 Corinthians 11:7–9)**. And moved by God's grace, the Macedonian believers, out of their poverty, contributed generously to the collection Paul was gathering for the poor Jewish church in Judea (**2 Corinthians 8:1–5**). A warm relationship developed between Paul and the believers in Philippi.

At the time of the writing of Philippians, Paul was in prison (**Philippians 1:13**). The traditional view is that Paul wrote this letter while imprisoned in Rome, along with the other captivity letters—Colossians, Philemon, and Ephesians. While some scholars have proposed other circumstances for the writing of Philippians, the evidence found in Philippians seems to best fit with the traditional view that Paul was imprisoned in Rome. Paul expressed optimism that he might soon be released (**Philippians 1:25; 2:24**), which might indicate that the book of Philippians was written toward the end of his imprisonment, around A.D. 61.

The Philippian believers heard about Paul's imprisonment and again sent him support in the form of gifts (probably of money) and in the form of a man named Epaphroditus (**Philippians 2:25; 4:18**).

Read about Paul's Roman imprisonment in **Acts 28:17–31**. Then read **Philippians 1:1–11**.

3. Paul describes himself and Timothy as servants (in Greek this word literally means "slaves") of Christ Jesus (**1:1**). Paul addresses the believers in Philippi as saints, that is, as those who have been made holy. How have they been made holy?

4. Paul's greeting (**1:2**) is really a blessing. Why are grace and peace such important blessings for Christians (see **Ephesians 2:8–9; John 14:27**; and **Philippians 4:6–7**)? Note Paul's coupling of Jesus with God the Father. God the Father and God the Son are the source of these blessings.

5. What is the reason for Paul's joy as he prays for the Philippians (1:4–5)? Of what might Paul be thinking?

6. The good work to which Paul refers in **1:6** is salvation; this good work is evidenced by the Philippians' partnership with Paul in the Gospel. In whom does Paul place his confidence that this good work of salvation would be brought to completion in the Philippians (**1:6**)? How does **1:7** support Paul's point? What do these verses say about who is responsible for salvation from beginning to end?

7. Compare **Philippians 1:9** with **Colossians 1:8–9.** Christian love is more than sentiment. What needs to inform that love?

8. What does Paul pray will result as love informed by knowledge and insight abounds in the lives of the Philippians (**1:10–11**)? Who is the source of their righteousness? What is the ultimate goal of living righteous lives, that is, of sanctification?

The Word for Us

1. Reread **Philippians 1:4–5.** With whom are you partners in the Gospel? Following Paul's example, how might you regard these people?

2. Reread **1:6.** In whom do we place our confidence for salvation?

3. Reread **1:9–11.** There is a strong cognitive element in Christianity. Our faith and the working out of our faith in love is not based primarily on emotion, though emotions such as joy do have a place in the Christian life (see **1:4**). Where do we find the knowledge that informs our love and directs our righteous acts? Use this prayer of Paul as you pray for others, especially your partners in the Gospel.

Closing

Read or sing together "May God Embrace Us with His Grace":

May God embrace us with His grace,
Pour blessings from His fountains,
And by the brightness of His face
Guide toward celestial mountains,

So that His saving acts we see
Wherein His love takes pleasure.
Let Jesus' healing power be
Revealed in richest measure,
Converting ev'ry nation.

All people living on His globe,
Praise God with exultation!
The world puts on a festive robe
And sings its jubilation
That Your rule, Lord, is strong and true
And curbs sin's evil hour.
Your Word stands guard and will renew
Your people's health and power
To live, Lord, in Your presence.

Our praises grow from living roots
When we thank God by action,
Improve the field, grow righteous fruits
Drawn by the Word's attraction.
Oh, bless us, Father and the Son
And Spirit, ever holy.
May people ev'rywhere be won
To love and praise You truly.
To this our heart-felt amen.

Lesson 2

Living and Dying for Christ (Philippians 1:12–26)

Theme Verse
"To me, to live is Christ and to die is gain" **(Philippians 1:21).**

Goal
We seek to live for Christ and look forward to being with Him after we die.

What's Going On Here?
In this section of Philippians Paul updates his partners in the Gospel in Philippi about how his imprisonment has benefited the Gospel. He shares with them his desire to glorify Christ whether he lives or dies.

Searching the Scriptures
1. Read **Philippians 1:12–14.** Having heard of Paul's imprisonment, the Philippians are no doubt concerned about the effect that imprisonment is having not only upon Paul but upon Paul's ministry. Paul reassures them that his imprisonment has served to advance the Gospel. How do the two developments Paul cites illustrate his point?

2. Read **1:15–17.** Paul's presence in Rome inspired two opposite reactions among those proclaiming the Gospel there. What two motives characterized these people?

3. Read **1:18.** What is Paul's reaction to these two groups?

4. Read **1:19–20.** What is the reason for Paul's joy? What is the shame Paul expects and hopes he will not experience (see **Mark 8:38**)? (In the Bible, the word *hope* refers to confidence, not wishful thinking **[Romans 8:24–25; Hebrews 11:1].**) From where does Paul receive the help that gives him courage (see also **Matthew 10:18–20**)?

5. Read **Philippians 1:21–26.** Compare **1:21** to **Galatians 2:20.** What does Paul mean when he says, "To live is Christ" **(Philippians 1:21)?** (See also **Romans 6:1–11.**)

6. Describe the conflicting desires that tear at Paul's heart (**Philippians 1:21–24**).

7. Reread **1:25–26.** Although Paul knows that the Lord alone will decide whether he lives or dies, he feels that the Lord still wants him to minister to the Philippians. What outcome does Paul foresee if he does indeed remain alive?

The Word for Us

1. Read **Romans 8:28,** which summarizes what Paul found to be true with regard to his imprisonment. Cite examples from your life or the life of someone else that illustrates the truth of this verse.

2. When envy and rivalry motivate people in the church, it can be a source of distress for others. However, what can we learn from Paul about how to regard such motives (see **Philippians 1:17–18**)?

3. What does **1:19–20** say about one of our most important tasks as partners with others in the Gospel? For whom can and should you fulfill this task?

4. How can we model Paul's attitude toward life and death in **Philippians 1:21–26?**

Closing

Read or sing together these stanzas of "For Me to Live Is Jesus":

For me to live is Jesus,
To die is gain for me;
So, when my Savior pleases,
I meet death willingly.

For Christ, my Lord, my brother,
I leave this world so dim
And gladly seek another,
Where I shall be with Him.

In my last hour, oh, grant me
A slumber soft and still,
No doubts to vex or haunt me,
Safe anchored in Your will;

This anchor of Your making
Forever holding me,
I will, in heav'n awaking,
Sing heaven's melody.

Lesson 3

United in Christ
as Humble Servants
(Philippians 1:27-2:11)

Theme Verses

"[Christ Jesus] made Himself nothing, taking the very nature of a servant, being made in human likeness. And being found in appearance as a man, He humbled Himself and became obedient to death—even death on a cross" **(Philippians 2:7–8)**!

Goal

Motivated by Jesus' service to us, we seek to serve humbly each other and strive in unity for the faith of the Gospel.

What's Going On Here?

Paul's concern in this section is the unity of the Philippians in the face of opposition. As he exhorts them to be united in spirit and in contending for the Gospel, he reminds them of the benefits of their salvation. And in a marvelous confession of faith, Paul holds up Christ as a powerful motivation for Christians to live as humble servants of each another, which in turn enables them to live in Christian unity.

Searching the Scriptures

1. Read **Philippians 1:27–28.** Whatever will happen with Paul, his main concern is the Gospel and those whose lives have been transformed by it. The verb in the phrase "conduct yourselves in a manner worthy of the gospel" **(1:27)** literally means "exercise citizenship." Many of the Philippi-

ans are no doubt quite proud of their Roman citizenship. Of what is Paul reminding them and what is he calling them to do?

2. The Philippians are not experiencing persecution as is Paul, but they are facing opposition. Whether in person or by word of mouth, Paul wants to hear a good report about their response to that opposition. What response does Paul counsel? What will that response show?

3. Read **Philippians 1:29–30.** How can Christians regard suffering for Christ as a gift given by God? (See **Matthew 5:11–12; Acts 5:41; James 1:2–3; 1 Peter 4:14.**)

Paul knew that divisiveness in the Philippian congregation would weaken its ability to persevere in the face of opposition. So earlier he exhorted them to "stand firm in one spirit, contending as one man for the faith of the gospel" **(1:27).** Now he expands on that thought. Read **Philippians 2:1–4.**

4. What motivation does Paul give for the conduct he urges in **2:2–4?**

5. **Philippians 2:2** is the heart of Paul's concern. What characterizes those who have been united with Christ? What practical steps does Paul give in **2:3–4** to achieve that end?

Selfishness is the essence of our sinful nature and something we struggle to overcome our entire lives. Paul holds up Jesus as the model of true unselfishness and the source of power for us in becoming like Him. The more we know Christ, the more we grow in being like Him. Read **2:5–11.** Because of its poetic structure, **2:6–11** is thought by some scholars to be a hymn that was sung in the early church. It contains a beautiful statement of Christ's person and work.

6. What does **2:6** say about the nature of Jesus?

7. Although He is God, what did Jesus not do **(2:6)?** What did He do **(2:7–8)?**

8. While the first part of the confession describes Jesus' humiliation, the second describes His exaltation. Reread **2:9–11.** What did God the Father do for Jesus (see also **Hebrews 1:3**)? What will the response of *all* creatures one day be? What will be the result of their response?

9. Compare **Philippians 2:10** with **Isaiah 45:20–25.** What does this comparison say about Jesus?

The Word for Us

1. God has given His people different gifts and in varying amounts. Some people are more talented than others in certain areas. Some are in positions where their gifts are used more visibly and they receive more praise and recognition than others. If we are not careful, that can be a source of divisiveness in the church as some people envy others and jockey for prestigious positions. Reread **Philippians 2:3.** How are we to treat others, whether their gifts are seemingly superior or inferior to ours? According to **1:27** what is to be our main concern?

2. Reread **2:6–8.** Why is this such a powerful motivation for us to live as humble, unselfish servants?

Closing

Read or sing together these stanzas of "O Christ, Our Hope":

O Christ, our hope, our hearts' desire,
Creation's mighty Lord,
Redeemer of the fallen world,
By holy love outpoured:

How vast Your mercy to accept
The burden of our sin
And bow Your head in cruel death
To make us clean within.

But now the bonds of death are burst,
The ransom has been paid;
You now ascend the Father's throne
In robes of light arrayed.

Oh, let Your mighty love prevail
To purge us of our pride
That we may stand before Your throne
By mercy purified.

Christ Jesus, be our present joy,
Our future great reward;
Our only glory, may it be
To glory in the Lord!

All praise to You, ascended Lord;
All glory ever be
To Father, Son, and Holy Ghost
Through all eternity!

Lesson 4

We Work Because God Works in Us (Philippians 2:12–30)

Theme Verses

"Continue to work out your salvation with fear and trembling, for it is God who works in you to will and to act according to His good purpose" **(Philippians 2:12–13).**

Goal

We seek to mature and persevere in the faith, shining like stars in the darkness of this world and holding out to others the Gospel of life.

What's Going On Here?

Paul continues to urge the Philippians to live in a way that befits the Gospel. He encourages them to work their salvation out to the finish, that is, to grow and persevere in the faith and produce its fruits. They can do this, he says, because God is working in them.

He fills them in on his plans to receive news from them and, he is confident, to see them in person soon. He commends Timothy to them as a future messenger, and he bids them to welcome and honor Epaphroditus, their messenger, whom he is sending back to them.

Searching the Scriptures

1. Read **Philippians 2:12–13.** What does Paul mean by "continue to work out your salvation" (see **Hebrews 3:14; 2 Peter 1:3–11**)? What does

he not mean (see **Ephesians 2:1, 4–5**)?

2. What is the relationship of God's working (**Philippians 2:13**) to our working (**2:12;** see also **2 Peter 1:3**)? What does God work in us?

3. Read **Philippians 2:14–16.** As in **1 Corinthians 10:10** Paul may have in mind the negative example of the Israelites in the wilderness, who grumbled against God incessantly. How were the lives of the Philippians to contrast with the world around them? What were they to offer others in the world?

4. What added incentive does Paul use in **Philippians 2:16** to encourage the Philippians to thus shine like stars in the universe?

5. Read **2:17–18.** Paul considers the fruit of the Philippians' faith to be a sacrifice to God (see **Romans 12:1**). The daily sacrifices commanded by God in the Old Testament were accompanied by drink offerings of wine **(Exodus 29:38–41).** Paul likely is referring to the fact that his trial might still result in his martyrdom when he says that he might be poured out as a drink offering accompanying their sacrifice of service. What attitude toward that possibility does he have and what does he urge the Philippians to copy?

6. Read **Philippians 2:19–24.** Paul is anxious to learn how things are going with the Philippians. He has chosen Timothy to travel to Philippi, visit them, and report back to him. However, until he knows the outcome of his trial, Paul has need of Timothy in Rome. So he has decided to wait until the outcome is known. That way when Timothy does travel to Philippi, he also can carry with him the news of how Paul's trial came out. What does Paul say about Timothy? With whom does he contrast Timothy? Of what outcome is he confident?

7. Read **Philippians 2:25–30.** How does Paul put the interests of Epaphroditus and the Philippians above his own interests? How was the mercy of God manifested to Epaphroditus and to Paul?

8. Although Epaphroditus' mission may have turned out differently than the Philippians anticipated, how are they to treat him?

The Word for Us

1. Reread **Philippians 2:12**. What things threaten our salvation (see **Hebrews 3:13; 1 Peter 5:8–9**)? What important things can we do to take advantage of the gifts our Lord has given us to strengthen and preserve us in the faith (see **Acts 2:42; Hebrews 10:25; Colossians 3:16**)?

2. Like the Philippians sent Epaphroditus to minister to Paul on their behalf, we send missionaries, evangelists, and others to go to places that we cannot go and to minister to the people of those places on our behalf. What can we learn from Paul's admonition in **Philippians 2:29–30** about how to regard and treat such people?

Closing

Read or sing together these stanzas of "Rise! To Arms! With Prayer Employ You":

Rise! To arms! With prayer employ you,
O Christians, lest the foe destroy you;
For Satan has designed your fall.
Wield God's Word, the weapon glorious;
Against all foes be thus victorious.
God will set you above them all.
Fear not the hordes of hell,
Here is Emmanuel.
Hail the Savior!
The strong foes yield
To Christ, our shield,
And we, the victors, hold the field.

Cast afar this world's vain pleasure
And boldly strive for heav'nly treasure.
Be steadfast in the Savior's might.
Trust the Lord, who stands beside you,
For Jesus from all harm will hide you.
By faith you conquer in the fight.
Take courage, weary soul!
Look forward to the goal!
Joy awaits you.
The race well run,
Your long war won,
Your crown shines splendid as the sun.

Wisely fight, for time is fleeting;
The hours of grace are fast retreating;
Short, short is this our earthly way.
When the Lord the dead will waken
And sinners all by fear are shaken,
The saints with joy will greet that day.
Praise God, our triumph's sure.
We need not long endure
Scorn and trial.
Our Savior King
His own will bring
To that great glory which we sing.

Lesson 5

Righteousness from God through Faith in Christ (Philippians 3:1–4:1)

Theme Verses

"What is more, I consider everything a loss compared to the surpassing greatness of knowing Christ Jesus my Lord, for whose sake I have lost all things. I consider them rubbish, that I may gain Christ and be found in Him, not having a righteousness of my own that comes from the law, but that which is through faith in Christ—the righteousness that comes from God and is by faith" **(Philippians 3:8–9)**.

Goal

Like Paul, we seek to be found in Christ, not having a righteousness of our own but the righteousness that God gives through faith in Christ.

What's Going On Here?

Paul warns the Philippians against those who teach that Christians must keep the Jewish ceremonial law in addition to trusting in Christ. Paul recounts the many things in which he could boast if such things did earn favor with God. But they do not, and in fact Paul now considers the things in which he formerly trusted as spiritual liabilities because they had blinded him to his need for the righteousness that only God can supply. Paul wants only to be found in Christ, having not his own supposed righteousness but the righteousness that God gives through faith in Christ.

Paul continues by describing how he strives as an athlete to gain the prize for which God has called him heavenward. He urges the Philippians to follow his example, warns them against those whose mind is set on earthly things, and calls them to remember their heavenly citizenship and stand firm in the Lord.

Searching the Scriptures

Read **Philippians 3:1–3**. The opponents Paul warns the Philippians to watch out for (apparently not for the first time) often are called Judaizers. These people were Jewish or Gentile converts to Christianity who insisted that in addition to faith in Christ, believers had to observe ceremonial laws from the Old Testament. They were especially insistent that believers must be circumcised. The net effect of their teaching was to say that people had to add obedience to these Old Testament laws to the work of Christ in order to be saved. This heresy troubled the churches in Galatia and Corinth and was condemned by the apostles in a council in Jerusalem (**Acts 15**).

Paul's condemnation of them in **Philippians 3:2** is full of irony. *Dogs* was a term used by Jews to refer to Gentiles, who were outside the covenant community and thus considered unclean. The Judaizers thought of themselves as the true extension of the Old Testament covenant community, as doers of good works (because of their insistence on following Old Testament laws), and as strict adherents of circumcision. Instead, Paul says that they are dogs, that is, they are outside the covenant community. He further notes that their works are evil, not good, and that their circumcision has no religious significance and is thus nothing but mutilation.

1. In contrast, how does Paul characterize the believers in Philippi (**Philippians 3:3**; see also **Romans 2:28–29; John 4:22–24; Acts 2:1–4, 14–18; Galatians 5:1–6**)?

If one could place confidence for salvation in conformity to Old Testament Law (as Paul himself thought before his conversion to Christianity), then Paul had every reason for such confidence. Read **Philippians 3:4–6.**

Unlike some of the Judaizers, who were converts to Judaism, Paul was born a Jew. And he was born into the tribe of Benjamin, one of the two tribes (along with Judah) that returned from captivity and was not lost to history. Not only was Paul born into a solidly Jewish family, he became a Pharisee. The Pharisees diligently studied the Old Testament and strictly adhered to their interpretation of Old Testament Law. Paul was so zealous for Judaism that he persecuted Christians. And by any observable standard, Paul had faithfully kept the Law.

2. Read **Philippians 3:7–9. Verses 7–8** consist of a series of progressively intense statements. In them Paul describes what he now thinks of those things in which he once took such confidence. How does Paul now regard them?

3. Reread **3:9.** Where does Paul want to be found? Why?

4. Read **3:10–11.** What is Paul's goal (see also **Ephesians 1:17–20; 2 Corinthians 4:6–13**)?

5. Read **Philippians 3:12–14.** What is the prize, the goal of the Christian life? When do believers attain it? In the meantime, how do they pursue it? To what are they responding as they do this, that is, what motivates and empowers them?

6. Read **Philippians 3:15–19.** Why are the Philippians to look to Paul as an example to follow (see also **1 Corinthians 11:1**)? How does Paul characterize those who live as enemies of the cross of Christ? What will be their end?

7. Read **Philippians 3:20–4:1?** In contrast to the enemies Paul described in **3:19,** on what are the Philippians to focus? To what are they to look forward? What are they to do in the meantime?

The Word for Us

1. Satan is always looking for ways to keep us from trusting Jesus alone for salvation. What things besides Jesus and His righteousness might we be tempted to think give us a more favorable standing in God's sight? What perspective should we have on those things according to **Philippians 3:4–9?**

2. Reread **3:17.** Whose example in the faith do you follow? What kind of example do you set?

Closing

Read or sing together these stanzas of "Salvation unto Us Has Come":

Salvation unto us has come
By God's free grace and favor;
Good works cannot avert our doom,
They help and save us never.
Faith looks to Jesus Christ alone,
Who did for all the world atone;
He is our one redeemer.

It was a false, misleading dream
That God His Law had given

That sinners could themselves redeem
And by their works gain heaven.
The Law is but a mirror bright
To bring the inbred sin to light
That lurks within our nature.

Faith clings to Jesus' cross alone
And rests in Him unceasing;
And by its fruits true faith is known,
With love and hope increasing.
For faith alone can justify;
Works serve our neighbor and supply
The proof that faith is living.

Lesson 6

Content in the Lord
(Philippians 4:2–23)

Theme Verses

"I know what it is to be in need, and I know what it is to have plenty. I have learned the secret of being content in any and every situation, whether well fed or hungry, whether living in plenty or in want. I can do everything through Him who gives me strength" **(Philippians 4:12–13)**.

Goal

We seek to be content in the Lord in all circumstances, turning over to Him all our anxieties in prayer with thanksgiving, that His peace may guard our hearts and minds in Christ.

What's Going On Here?

In his final exhortations, Paul touches on a number of issues that he has previously discussed: Christian unity; joy in the Lord; gentleness toward others; following his example. Paul also thanks the Philippians for their concern for him and for their gifts. And he shares the secret of being content in all circumstances: trusting in the Lord for strength. He assures the Philippians that God will meet all of their needs out of His glorious riches in Christ, and He blesses them with the grace of the Lord Jesus.

Searching the Scriptures

Read **Philippians 4:2–3.** Paul here takes the unusual step of admonishing two individuals by name. Apparently, he considers their dispute to have serious consequences, and he considers them mature enough to handle the admonition.

1. On what basis does Paul plead with these women to agree with each other? How does he refer to them? Do others have a role to play in helping them to resolve the dispute? At the end of **verse 3,** Paul mentions an important thing that all believers have in common and that can lend some much-needed perspective to the dispute. What is it?

2. Read **4:4–7.** Reread **verse 4.** What effect do outward circumstances have on the believer's joy? In whom is that joy rooted?

3. According to **4:5** what should characterize our dealings with all others (see also **2:3–4**)? The Lord may return at any time, and from the perspective of eternity, His return is near. How can that affect our attitude and how we treat others?

4. In **4:6,** what does Paul urge as an antidote for anxiety? What important element should accompany petitions in prayer?

5. As those who are in union with Christ Jesus do what Paul encourages, what will result **(4:7)**? How does Paul describe God's peace?

6. Read **Philippians 4:8–9.** Where are our thoughts to be fixed? What are we to put into practice? What promise sustains us?

7. Read **4:10–13.** The Philippians had sent Paul gifts (probably of money) for his physical support by the hand of Epaphroditus. Paul is grateful for the gifts and touched by the generosity of the Philippians. Nonetheless, he wants to make clear that his contentment does not lie in earthly possessions. Where does it lie?

8. Read **4:14–20.** Paul rejoices **(4:10)** not only because the Philippians have given him gifts but more importantly because of what those gifts say about the Philippians. How are the gifts regarded in God's sight **(4:18)?** Even if the Philippians had to sacrifice to send the gifts, why should they not worry **(4:19)?** What overflows from Paul's heart as he contemplates the truth of **4:19 (4:20)?**

9. Read **4:21–23.** What blessing does Paul pronounce on all who read this letter **(4:23)?**

The Word for Us

1. Disputes among brothers and sisters in the faith can tear apart congregations and cause the wasting of valuable time and resources. How can remembering the great spiritual riches we share in Christ, our unity in Christ, the importance of proclaiming the Gospel, and the fact that we will spend eternity together help us resolve disputes?

2. Discuss ways of reminding yourself and each other of what Paul says in **4:4–7.**

3. What we allow into our minds and what we concentrate our thoughts on—these things have an enormous impact on our behavior. How do Paul's words in **4:8–9** apply to what we read, watch, and listen to? How can doing what Paul says in these verses impact our relationships with other people, especially people we may not particularly like?

4. How can we, like Paul, learn the secret of contentment, no matter what our earthly circumstances **(4:12–13, 19)?**

Closing

Read or sing together these stanzas of "God Brought Me to This Time and Place":

God brought me to this time and place
Surrounded by His favor.
He guarded all my nights and days,
His kindness did not waver.
His peace as sentinel He gave
My spirit's health and joy to save.
To this day He has blessed me.

All honor, thanks, and praise to You,
O Father, God of heaven,
For mercies ev'ry morning new,
Which You have freely given.
Inscribe this on my memory:
My Lord has done great things for me;
To this day He has helped me.

Oh, help me ever, God of grace,
Through ev'ry time and season,
At ev'ry turn, in ev'ry place—
Redemptive love the reason.
Through joy and pain and final breath
By Jesus' life and saving death
Help me as You have helped me.

PHILIPPIANS
Joy in Christ

Leaders Notes

Preparing to Teach Philippians

The materials in these notes are designed to help you in leading others through this portion of the Holy Scriptures. Nevertheless, this booklet is to be an aid to and not a substitute for your own study of and preparation for teaching the book of Philippians.

If you have the opportunity, you will find it helpful to make use of other biblical reference works in the course of your study. The following contains a helpful commentary on the book of Philippians: *Philippians, Colossians, Philemon*, The People's Bible, by Harlyn J. Kuschel (Milwaukee: Northwestern Publishing House, 1986; reprinted by Concordia Publishing House, St. Louis, 1992). Although it is not strictly a commentary, the section on Paul's captivity letters, including Philippians, in *The Word of the Lord Grows* by Martin H. Franzmann (St. Louis: Concordia, 1961) also contains information that is of value for interpreting this biblical book.

Group Bible Study

Group Bible study means mutual learning from one another under the guidance of a leader. The Bible is an inexhaustible resource. No one person can discover all it has to offer. In a class many eyes see many things and can apply them to many life situations. The leader should resist the temptation to "give the answers" and so act as an "authority." This teaching approach stifles participation by individual members and can actually hamper learning. As a general rule the teacher is not to "give interpretation" but to "develop interpreters." Of course there are times when the leader should and must share insights and information gained by his or her own deeper research. The ideal class is one in which the leader guides class members through the lesson and engages them in meaningful sharing and discussion at all points, leading them to a summary of the lesson at the close. As a general rule, don't explain what the learners can discover by themselves.

Have a chalkboard and chalk or newsprint and marker available to emphasize significant points of the lesson. Rephrase your inquiries or the inquiries of participants as questions, problems, or issues. This provokes thought. Keep discussion to the point. List on the chalkboard or newsprint the answers given. Then determine the most vital points made in the discussion. Ask additional questions to fill gaps.

The aim of every Bible study is to help people grow spiritually, not merely in biblical and theological knowledge, but in Christian thinking and living. This means growth in Christian attitudes, insights, and skills for Christian living. The focus of this course must be the church and the world of our day. The guiding question will be this: What does the Lord teach us for life today through the book of Philippians?

Pace Your Teaching

The lessons in this course of study are designed for a study session of at least an hour in length. If it is the desire and intent of the class to complete an entire lesson each session, it will be necessary for you to keep careful watch over the class time. At times it may be necessary for you to summarize the content of certain answers or biblical references in order to preserve time. Asking various class members to look up different Bible passages and to read them aloud to the rest of the class will save time over having every class member look up each reference.

Also, you may not want to cover every question in each lesson. This may lead to undue haste and frustration. Be selective. Pace your teaching. Spend no more than 5–10 minutes with "Theme Verse," "Goal," and "What's Going On Here?" Take time to go into the text by topic, but not word by word. Get the sweep of meaning. Occasionally stop to help the class gain understanding of a word or concept. Allow approximately 10–15 minutes for "The Word for Us." Allowing approximately 5 minutes for "Closing" and announcements, you will notice, allows you only approximately 30 minutes for "Searching the Scriptures."

Should your group have more than a one-hour class period, you can take it more leisurely. But do not allow any lesson to drag and become tiresome. Keep it moving. Keep it alive. Keep it meaningful. Eliminate some questions and restrict yourself to those questions most meaningful to the members of the class. If most members study the text at home, they can report their findings, and the time gained can be applied to relating the lesson to life.

Good Preparation

Good preparation by the leader usually affects the pleasure and satisfaction the class will experience.

Suggestions to the Leader for Using the Study Guide

The Lesson Pattern

This set of six lessons is based on a timely New Testament book—Philippians. The material is designed to aid *Bible study*, that is, to aid a consideration of the written Word of God, with discussion and personal application growing out of the text at hand.

The typical lesson is divided into these sections:

1. Theme Verse
2. Goal
3. What's Going On Here?
4. Searching the Scriptures
5. The Word for Us
6. Closing

"Theme Verse," "Goal," and "What's Going On Here?" give the leader assistance in arousing the interest of the group in the concepts of the lesson. Here the leader stimulates minds. Do not linger too long over the introductory remarks.

"Searching the Scriptures" provides the real spadework necessary for Bible study. Here the class digs, uncovers, and discovers; it gets the facts and observes them. Comments from the leader are needed only to the extent that they help the group understand the text. The questions in this guide, corresponding to sections within the text, are intended to help the participants discover the meaning of the text.

Having determined what the text says, the class is ready to apply the message. Having heard, read, marked, and learned the Word of God, proceed to digest it inwardly through discussion, evaluation, and application. This is done, as this guide suggests, by taking the truths found in Philippians and applying them to the world and Christianity in general and then to personal Christian life. Class time may not permit discussion of all questions and topics. In preparation the leader may need to select one or two and focus on them. These questions bring God's message to the individual Christian. Close the session by reviewing one important truth from the lesson.

Remember, the Word of God is sacred, but this study guide is not. The notes in this section offer only guidelines and suggestions. Do not hesitate to alter the guidelines or substitute others to meet your needs and the needs of the participants. Adapt your teaching plan to your class and your class period. Good teaching directs the learner to discover for himself or herself. For the teacher this means directing the learner, not giving the learner answers. Choose the verses that should be looked up in Scripture. What discussion questions will you ask? At what points? Write them in the margin of your study guide. Involve class members, but give them clear directions. What practical actions might you propose for the week following the lesson? Which of the items do you consider most important for your class?

How will you best use your teaching period? Do you have 45 minutes? an hour? or an hour and a half? If time is short, what should you cut? Learn to become a wise steward of class time.

Be sure to take time to summarize the lesson, or have a class member do it. Plan a brief opening devotion, using members of the class.

Remember to pray frequently for yourself and your class. May God the Holy Spirit bless your study and your leading of others into the comforting truths of God's Christ-centered Word.

Lesson 1

Partners in the Gospel

The Class Session

Have volunteers read "Theme Verses," "Goal," and "What's Going On Here?"

Searching the Scriptures

1. After having a vision of a man from Macedonian begging him to come and help the people there, Paul and his companions concluded that the Lord was calling them to preach the Gospel in Macedonia, and so they quickly obeyed (**Acts 16:9–10**).

2. Lydia, who previously was a worshiper of God but not a full-fledged convert to Judaism, and the members of her household, along with the jailer and the members of his household, were among the members of the church in Philippi. Timothy was among Paul's companions during this visit.

3. The believers in Philippi have been made holy by being "in Christ Jesus," that is, united with Him by faith.

4. God's unmerited favor led Him to send Jesus to purchase our forgiveness by dying on the cross. Grace also moved God to give us the gift of faith to trust in what Jesus did for our salvation. To those who trust in Him for salvation Jesus promises the peace of mind and heart that comes from knowing that their sins are forgiven and they now have peace with God (**Romans 5:1**). The grace of God is the source of our salvation, and the peace of God undergirds and guards us in the midst of the anxieties of this life.

5. The partnership that the Philippians have with Paul in the Gospel is the reason for his joy. Paul is likely thinking of the support he has received from the Philippians, both materially and spiritually, which God has used to strengthen, encourage, and provide for him that he might continue proclaiming the Gospel.

6. Paul places his confidence not in the Philippians themselves but in God who began the good work of salvation in them and would bring it to completion. In **1:7** Paul notes that he and the Philippians share God's

grace, which makes possible not only their salvation but the proclamation of the Gospel in which they are partners. These verses clearly indicate that God alone is responsible for salvation.

7. Christian love is informed by knowledge of God's will and practical insight into how that is lived out.

8. Paul prays that the Philippians will be able to discern what is best. This is important for their spiritual preservation and growth as they are faced with religious teachings and with ethical choices. Paul prays that they will be pure and blameless until Christ's return, filled with the fruit of righteousness. The source of that righteousness and its fruit is Jesus Christ. Sanctification in the lives of His people results in God receiving the praise and glory.

The Word for Us

1. Answers will vary. Many people would consider themselves to be partners in the Gospel with their pastor and the other members of their congregation, with others in their church body, and with missionaries who they might support. As we pray for our partners in the Gospel we can, along with Paul, pray with joy because of their partnership with us in the great work of spreading the Good News of salvation.

2. We place our confidence in God who brought us to faith and will bring that good work to completion. This does not mean, however, that people can willfully turn their back on God's salvation. Read this comment on **Philippians 1:6** by Harlyn J. Kuschel:

> The apostle certainly is not advocating overconfidence here. Nor is he implying that once a person has been brought to faith he cannot lose the blessings God has given. In the very next chapter he urges believers to use diligently the spiritual weapons and powers the Lord has given them to fight against sin and temptation and to grow in faith. But here Paul is encouraging believers with God's own promise. God graciously brings believers to faith and assures them that, as they continue to use his word and the sacraments, he will preserve them in faith. Christians' spiritual security, therefore, does not depend on their own sin-tainted efforts. It rests on the promises and power of God. (*The People's Bible: Philippians, Colossians, Philemon* © 1986 Northwestern Publishing House, Milwaukee, WI. Used by permission.)

3. Knowledge of God's will (**Colossians 1:9**) is found in the Bible. Learning that knowledge and how to apply it is, as Paul indicates, something in which we grow throughout our Christian lives.

Closing

Follow the suggestion in the study guide.

Lesson 2

Living and Dying for Christ

The Class Session

Have volunteers read "Theme Verse," "Goal," and "What's Going On Here?"

Searching the Scriptures

1. The Gospel has been advanced as it has become known among the whole palace guard and indeed throughout the city that Paul is not a criminal but that he is imprisoned for preaching the Gospel. The palace guard consists of elite troops stationed in Rome, some of whom guard Caesar himself. Apparently others guard prisoners like Paul who are awaiting a trial before Caesar. Paul's imprisonment has given him the opportunity to witness to his guards, and word of the Gospel has spread throughout the palace guard and the city.

Paul's imprisonment has further served to advance the Gospel because God has used Paul's example to embolden the Christians in Rome to proclaim more fearlessly and courageously the Gospel.

2. Some proclaimed the Gospel out of love for Paul, realizing that the Lord put him where he was to defend the Gospel. Others were envious of Paul and preached Christ out of selfish ambition, perhaps seeking to elevate themselves above Paul.

3. Paul's primary concern is the Gospel, and he rejoices that the Gospel is being proclaimed, whether the motives behind the proclamation are true or false.

4. Paul's joy is rooted in his confidence that what has happened to him will result in his deliverance (literally, salvation; **1:19**) and in Christ being exalted through him (**1:20**)—no matter what the outcome of his trial. Should he be acquitted, he would be delivered from prison and Christ would be exalted in his life. Should he be sentenced to death, he would be delivered from this life and Christ would be exalted in his death.

Paul is confident that he will have sufficient courage to make a bold defense of the Gospel and will not be ashamed of and deny his association

---

with the Gospel and thus cause Jesus to be ashamed of him on Judgment Day.

Paul receives help through the prayers of fellow believers and through the Spirit, whom Jesus promised would give His people the words to say when they are in situations just like Paul's.

5. Believers have been crucified with Christ and thus have died to themselves and their sinful nature. Now Christ lives in them and works out His will in them and through them. However, until they die, Christians still have their sinful nature and will continue to sin. Thus, they should often remind themselves as they confess their sins that they have indeed died to sin in Christ and now live to Him.

6. On the one hand, Paul desires to die and be with Christ; this being with Christ would far surpass the union with Christ believers have in this life. On the other hand, Paul knows that if he continues to live it will be because the Lord has something yet for him to do, and Paul knows that the church he has planted in Philippi as well as others still need his wisdom and his guidance.

7. Paul is convinced that he will remain alive and that his continued ministry to the Philippians will result in their growth in the faith and in their joy in Christ overflowing because of him.

The Word for Us

1. Answers will vary.

2. Like Paul we are most concerned about the proclamation of the Gospel. While we may deplore the motives of envy and rivalry, we can rejoice when the Gospel is being proclaimed, even out of selfish motives.

3. **Philippians 1:19** notes the importance of the prayers of others in helping those who proclaim the Gospel to do so with courage even in the face of persecution and death. We need to pray for our church leaders, our family and friends, and believers worldwide, especially those who face persecution and death because they believe and proclaim the Gospel.

4. We can live our life to our Lord, knowing that He lives in us and works through us. We can be thankful for this life and for the tasks He has given us to do, even if they don't seem as important to the Gospel as the tasks given to Paul. And we can look forward to death and being with our Lord when He decides that our tasks for Him on this earth are finished.

Closing

Follow the suggestion in the study guide.

Lesson 3

United in Christ as Humble Servants

The Class Session

Have volunteers read "Theme Verses," "Goal," and "What's Going On Here?"

Searching the Scriptures

1. Paul is reminding the Philippians that they have a citizenship far more important than their Roman citizenship—they are citizens of God's kingdom. He is calling them to carry out that citizenship in a way that reflects the influence of the Gospel and that brings it honor, rather than disgrace.

2. Paul wants the Philippians to take a firm and united stand in contending for the Gospel and not be frightened by those who oppose them. This will testify to the power of God who enables such a bold, unwavering response and thus will signal to the opposition that they will be destroyed while the Philippian believers will be saved.

3. God's message and messengers have always been opposed by the evil one and those under his influence. Christians expect no better treatment than the prophets and Jesus Himself received. But more than that, Christians can rejoice when God considers them worthy of suffering for His name. They can trust that God has given them His Spirit and is using the suffering to work perseverance, which in turn works in them a mature faith. And they can look forward to the eternal rewards such suffering reaps.

4. In **Philippians 2:1** Paul motivates the Philippians by reminding them of the benefits of their salvation (that is, from their being "united with Christ," or literally, "in Christ"): encouragement from being united with Christ; comfort from knowing God's love for them in Christ (see **Romans 5:8**); fellowship with the Spirit; tenderness and compassion.

5. Those who have been united with Christ also have been united with each other and their lives are characterized by a common view of life as nurtured by the Scriptures, by love, and by singleness of purpose in contending for the Gospel (see **1:27**). This can be achieved as believers,

motivated by their union with Christ, do nothing out of selfish ambition or vain conceit, humbly consider others better than themselves, and take into account the interests of others as well as their own interests.

6. **Philippians 2:6** says that Jesus is God and is equal with God.

7. Scholars debate the nuances of **2:6b.** Some think it means that Jesus did not consider His glory with the Father before His incarnation as something to be held onto. That is, He was willing to put His glory aside when He became man. Others think the phrase means that He did not use His glory, power, and authority as God to His own advantage. That is, Jesus did not appear on earth in all His glory (as He did for a short while during His transfiguration), and He did not flaunt His power. In any case, the main point is clear: Jesus did not use His equality with God selfishly.

In contrast, Jesus made Himself nothing, literally, "emptied Himself." This does not mean that He gave up His divine nature, but that He laid aside its glory to become a man. He took on human flesh and became a servant. He humbled Himself and obeyed the Father's will that He die and not only that He die, but that He die a humiliating death, a kind of death that was cursed by God **(Galatians 3:13).**

8. God the Father exalted Jesus to the highest place of honor and gave Him a name above all names. *All* creatures in the universe will one day confess that Jesus is Lord. Believers will do so with faith and joy. Unbelievers and the demons will do so to their shame (see **Isaiah 45:23–24**). This confession of Jesus as Lord will result in God the Father being glorified.

9. The comparison of these passages further reinforces the truth that Jesus is God because He will receive the worship reserved for God alone.

The Word for Us

1. We are to give others preferential treatment. Our main concern is to share our faith in the Gospel.

2. If our Lord put aside the magnificent glory that is rightfully His to humble Himself, take on the form of a servant, and become obedient to a humiliating death—all to bring us salvation—how can we not give up our puny pretensions to glory in order to follow Him in humble service to others?

Closing

Follow the suggestion in the study guide.

Lesson 4

We Work Because God Works in Us

The Class Session

Have volunteers read "Theme Verses," "Goal," and "What's Going On Here?"

Searching the Scriptures

1. The following comments by Harlyn J. Kuschel explain what Paul means and does not mean by "continue to work out your salvation" **(Philippians 2:12):**

> Before they are brought to faith, human beings are totally incapable of any positive spiritual working. "As for you," Paul tells the Ephesian believers, "you were dead in your transgressions and sins" (Ephesians 2:1). But then he goes on, "But because of his great love for us, God, who is rich in mercy, made us alive with Christ" (2:4[–5]). When God saves sinners by bringing them to faith in Jesus through the gospel, he makes them spiritually alive in Christ. Believers are now capable of spiritual working and the spiritual effort Paul calls for in our text. This is not a working which earns, or tries to earn salvation. It is a working by which believers, who know that they have been saved by the blood of Christ, make the best use of their spiritual gifts and powers with which the Holy Spirit has supplied them to grow in faith, bring forth the fruits of faith, and remain steadfast in faith unto eternal life. (*The People's Bible: Philippians, Colossians, Philemon* © 1986 Northwestern Publishing House, Milwaukee, WI. Used by permission.)

2. It is because God works in us that we are able to do the spiritual work that Paul urges in **Philippians 2:12.** God works in us both the intentions and the actions to accomplish His good purpose.

3. As the Philippians willingly, without complaining or arguing, obeyed their Lord, their blameless and pure lives would contrast with the morally depraved world in which they lived. Moreover, because of their blameless

conduct and the word of life, that is the Gospel, that they were to hold out, they would be like stars shining in the universe.

4. Paul urges the Philippians to live blameless lives and hold out the word of life so that it will be evident on Judgment Day that he did not labor among them in vain.

5. Paul rejoices with the Philippians and urges them to rejoice with him that he and they are able to offer the sacrifice of holy lives dedicated to Christ and to the spreading of the Gospel, even if that means death for him.

6. Paul says that Timothy is genuinely concerned about the welfare of the Philippians. It is likely that others of Paul's most trusted companions (like Luke) were at that time away from Rome on other errands. Among those left in Rome, only Timothy had the spiritual maturity to put the interests of the Gospel above his own interests. Paul considers Timothy as a son who has served alongside him in the work of the Gospel. Paul is confident that he will be released and will himself be able to come to Philippi soon.

7. Paul undoubtedly could continue to benefit from the services of Epaphroditus in Rome. However, to allay the concerns of the Philippians about Epaphroditus' health and to allay Epaphroditus' concern about their concern, Paul sacrifices Epaphroditus' continued help and sends him back to Philippi, probably carrying this letter. God's mercy was manifested to Epaphroditus in that he recovered after being on the verge of death, and it was manifested to Paul in that he was spared the sorrow of having Epaphroditus die.

8. Although Epaphroditus' mission was cut short, the Philippians are to welcome him in the Lord with great joy and honor him for risking his life for the Gospel and for being their personal messenger to help Paul.

The Word for Us

1. Sin and Satan constantly seek to pull us away from the Lord. We can arm ourselves to work out our own salvation—that is, to bear spiritual fruit and remain faithful until the end of our lives or Christ's return—by gathering together with other believers and making use of the Word and the sacraments. All of the verses cited point to the gathering together of believers that is the church. In the church, believers gather to hear, read, study, and sing the Scriptures, receive the sacraments, pray for each other, and encourage each other to remain faithful as the day of our Lord's return approaches.

2. Whether or not things worked out the way we intended, we are to honor such people and welcome them when they return, rejoicing in how God used them on our behalf.

Closing

Follow the suggestion in the study guide.

Lesson 5

Righteousness from God through Faith in Christ

The Class Session

Have volunteers read "Theme Verses," "Goal," and "What's Going On Here?"

Searching the Scriptures

1. Paul characterizes the believers in Philippi as those who have true circumcision, circumcision of the heart. They live in the new era of salvation in which the Holy Spirit has been poured out on all God's people and moves them to worship God in spirit and truth. These believers look to Christ alone for salvation and put no confidence in things done to their flesh or by their flesh, that is, by their human nature.

2. For the sake of Christ, Paul now realizes that those things he once considered spiritual assets were really liabilities because they blinded him to his spiritual need for forgiveness and the righteousness that comes only through faith in Jesus. Compared to the surpassing greatness of knowing Christ Jesus his Lord, Paul considers to be a liability everything else in which he could mistakenly place his confidence. Indeed he has lost all such things and considers them rubbish or dung that he instead might gain Christ (see also **Matthew 16:26**).

3. Paul wants to be found in Christ. To be in union with Christ is the essence of salvation (see **Romans 8:1; 2 Corinthians 5:17**). When believers are united with Christ through faith, they receive His righteousness. Paul realizes that his own righteousness based on keeping the Law is worthless and that the only righteousness that counts in God's sight is that which is a gift from God and comes through faith in Christ. A person cannot have it both ways. Human "righteousness" and the righteousness that is given by God through faith are mutually exclusive.

4. Paul wants to know Christ better, not merely in a factual way, but in a relational way. Paul wants to experience the power of God that raised Jesus from the dead, the power that works in believers to bring them closer to Christ and transform them into His image. Paul is so closely identified with Jesus that he wants to share in His sufferings, that is, to suffer for the

sake of the Gospel. Paul's ultimate goal is to share in Christ's resurrection. In Baptism, believers have already in this life died with Christ and been raised with Him **(Romans 6:3–4)**, but Paul is looking forward to his physical resurrection from the dead. As we know from many passages such as **Philippians 1:23,** Paul is not uncertain of his salvation, but the final goal is not yet reached as Paul will go on to stress in the next passage.

5. The goal and prize is resurrection from the dead **(3:11)** and perfection **(3:12)**, the sinless life believers will live forever with Jesus. They will only attain this after they die, not in this life. But that doesn't mean they should think that it doesn't matter how they live here on earth. Instead, they strive for perfection as an athlete intently strives to win a race. They don't look back on any past accomplishments, thinking they can earn God's favor, nor do they look back at their past sins but instead trust in His forgiveness as they press ahead toward the goal. They do this in response to Jesus taking hold of them and God calling them heavenward in Jesus. Thus, it is the grace of God in Christ that motivates and empowers their striving to reach the goal of perfection.

6. The Philippians are to look to Paul as an example to follow because there are many who live as enemies of Jesus' cross and following their example would endanger the Philippians. Paul characterizes these enemies as those who selfishly focus on fulfilling their appetites to the point that these appetites have become their god. The things in which they glory will prove to be to their shame. Such people, says Paul, are focused exclusively on earthly things. Their end is destruction.

7. Rather than focusing on earthly things, the Philippians are to remember that they are citizens of heaven and look forward to the return of their Savior, who will transform their lowly bodies to be like His glorious body. They are to stand firm in the Lord as they await that day.

The Word for Us

1. Answers to the first question will vary. Participants might mention a Christian family, church membership, service they provide at church or in the community, wealth, status, profession. Like Paul, we should realize that as far as providing a favorable standing with God such things are worthless. And indeed, they can be spiritual liabilities that will shipwreck our faith if they turn us from looking to Christ alone for the righteousness God requires.

2. Answers will vary.

Closing

Follow the suggestion in the study guide.

Lesson 6

Content in the Lord

The Class Session

Have volunteers read "Theme Verses," "Goal," and "What's Going On Here?"

Searching the Scriptures

1. Paul pleads with these apparently prominent, influential women to agree with each other in the Lord, that is, to remember what they have in common in the Lord and put aside their differences for the much more important sake of the Gospel. Paul refers to these women as ones who have contended at his side in the cause of the Gospel. Paul asks another individual to help resolve the dispute. And he mentions other workers, bringing to mind the marvelous fellowship of those who have worked alongside him—a fellowship undoubtedly strained by this dispute. Finally, Paul mentions that the names of all of them are written in the book of life. That wonderful truth will help these women put their dispute in perspective and resolve it quickly.

2. Christian joy transcends changing circumstances because it is rooted in the Lord who does not change and in whom Christians have wonderful blessings that no circumstances can change (see also **Romans 8:35–39**).

3. Gentleness, or a forebearing attitude that humbly looks out for the interests of others, should characterize our dealings with all people. The nearness of the Lord's return can encourage us to rejoice in the Lord and can motivate us to have Christlike concern for others just as Paul encourages.

4. Rather than being anxious about anything, Paul urges Christians to pray, taking their concerns to God. Thanksgiving should accompany petitionary prayer.

5. As those who are "in Christ Jesus" (**4:7**) turn their anxieties over to the Lord in prayer, God's peace will act as a sentinel, guarding their hearts and minds. God's peace transcends human comprehension; it is beyond our understanding how we can experience that peace in all circumstances,

even in the midst of suffering.

6. Our thoughts are to be fixed on things that are true, noble, right, pure, lovely, admirable, excellent, and praiseworthy. We are to put into practice what we have learned from Paul. Obviously, we have never seen Paul in person, but there is much in his many New Testament letters that we can put into practice. Paul promises that the God of peace will be with us.

7. Paul's contentment, no matter what his earthly circumstances, lies in the Lord Jesus, who gives Paul the strength to meet all the challenges of life and to live his life for Him.

8. The gifts are seen by God as fragrant offerings that please Him; they are fruits of the faith of the Philippians. The Philippians need never worry about being generous because God will supply all that they need (physically and spiritually) from His glorious riches in Christ Jesus. That truth causes praise to God to well up in the heart of Paul.

9. Paul pronounces the blessing of the grace of the Lord Jesus on his readers. It is grace, God's undeserved favor, that brings people into a relationship with Him and keeps them in that relationship until they go to be with Him forever (4:9–11). From that grace flow all other blessings such as peace (4:7) and joy (4:4).

The Word for Us

1. Remembering these things can help us focus on what is really important to God and to us and help us see how important it is that nothing get in the way of the work of the Gospel.

2. Answers will vary.

3. We are wise if we use Paul's list as a criteria for judging what we read, see, and hear. Allowing our minds, even occasionally, to be filled with things opposite those Paul lists can profoundly damage our minds, our faith, our relationships, and the message of the Gospel.

Often when we do not like other people, we tend to focus on the things they do that annoy or hurt us. If we instead listen to Paul and focus on things about those people that are praiseworthy, our relationships with them might well improve.

4. Like Paul, we can trust Christ to give us the strength to cope with any situation. We can remember the vast spiritual treasures we have received in Him and trust God to meet all of our needs out of His glorious riches in Christ.

Closing

Follow the suggestion in the study guide.